GRAPHIC LIBRARY®

EST. CARTOON★NATION 1776

presents

U.S. IMMIGRATION

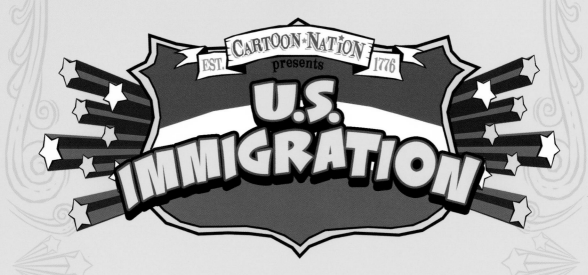

by Liam O'Donnell

illustrated by Charles Barnett III

CONSULTANT:

Michael Bailey

Colonel William J. Walsh Associate Professor

of American Government

Georgetown University, Washington, D.C.

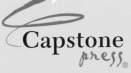

Capstone press®

Mankato, Minnesota

Graphic Library is published by Capstone Press,
151 Good Counsel Drive, P.O. Box 669, Mankato, Minnesota 56002.
www.capstonepress.com

1 2 3 4 5 6 13 12 11 10 09 08

Library of Congress Cataloging-in-Publication Data
O'Donnell, Liam, 1970–
    U.S. immigration / by Liam O'Donnell; illustrated by Charles Barnett III.
    p. cm. — (Graphic library. Cartoon nation)
    Summary: "In cartoon format, explains the history of U.S. immigration and describes
how immigrants have shaped the United States" — Provided by publisher.
    Includes bibliographical references and index.
    ISBN-13: 978-1-4296-1983-7 (hardcover)
    ISBN-10: 1-4296-1983-X (hardcover)
    ISBN-13: 978-1-4296-2855-6 (softcover pbk.)
    ISBN-10: 1-4296-2855-3 (softcover pbk.)
    1. United States — Emigration and immigration — History — Juvenile literature. I.
Barnett, Charles, III, ill. II. Title. III. Series.
JV6450.O63 2009
304.8'73 — dc22   2008000488

Art Director and Designer
Bob Lentz

Production Designer
Kim Brown

Colorist
Krista Ward

Cover Artist
Kelly Brown

Editor
Christopher L. Harbo

CARTOON NATION EST. 1776

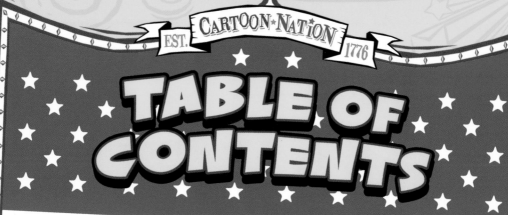

TABLE OF CONTENTS

Do you know an immigrant? You probably do, and it may even be you! Immigrants are people who leave their home country to become part of another nation.

Now that might not be you, but it's probably true of your great-great-great grandparents. Most U.S. citizens are descendants of people who immigrated to America. That's why the United States is known as a nation of immigrants.

Sometimes, the United States is called a "melting pot." Many immigrants combine traditions from their old country with traditions from America.

Pour in everything you can and this country will turn out great.

descendant — a person's child and a family member born after that child

Of course, not everyone in the United States can trace their ancestors back to another country. Native Americans have ancestors who were here thousands of years before the United States became a nation.

ancestor — a family member who lived a long time ago

People have been moving from one country to another for thousands of years. Today, immigration happens all over the world. It makes countries stronger and better places to live.

THE FIRST IMMIGRANTS

Some archaeologists believe the first people immigrated to North America 15,000 years ago. Others think the first immigrants arrived as far back as 40,000 years ago. Many believe they traveled across frozen land joining Siberia and Alaska. But others think the first immigrants arrived by boat along the western coastline.

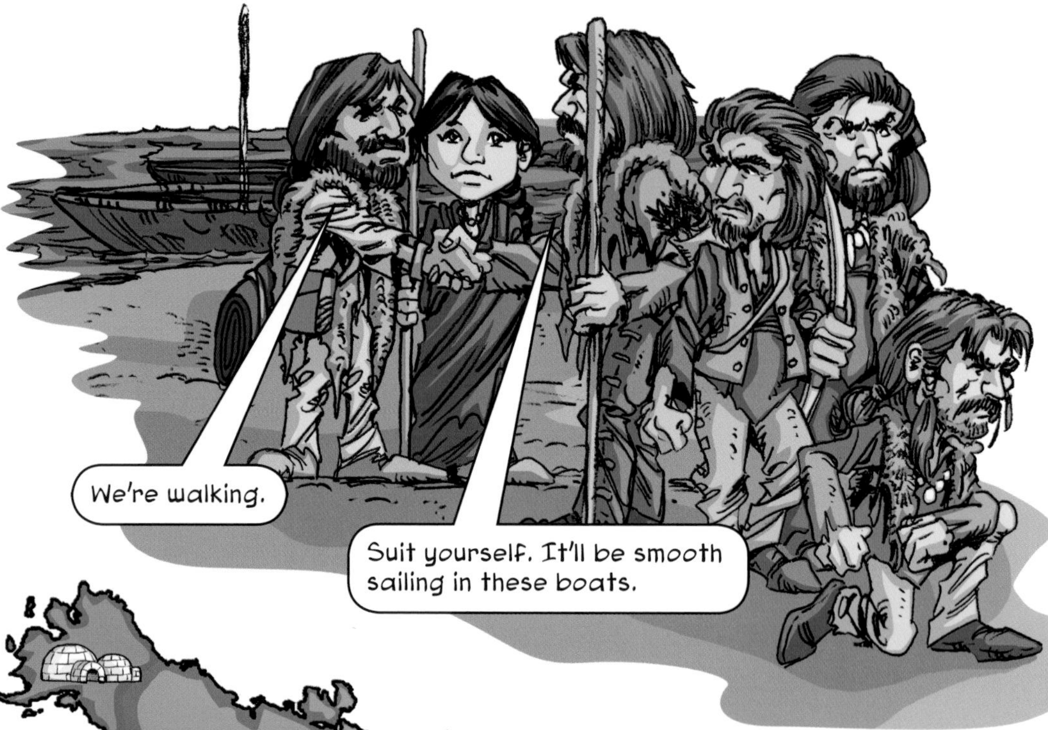
We're walking.
Suit yourself. It'll be smooth sailing in these boats.

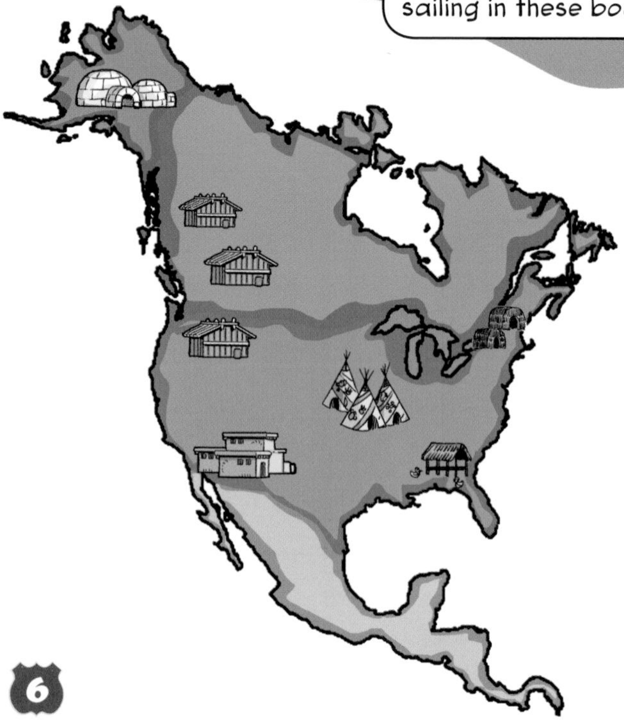

The first immigrants to North America eventually became the Native American nations. For thousands of years, Native Americans lived in North America by themselves. They developed their own civilizations and languages.

Around AD 1000, the second group of immigrants arrived in North America. Vikings from Scandinavia sailed to the area known today as Newfoundland, Canada. They built settlements and made contact with some of the Native American tribes.

According to Viking sagas, the Vikings lived in Newfoundland for only about 10 years. Colder winters and diseases may have made life too difficult for the Vikings. Eventually, they decided to sail back to their homelands in Scandinavia.

saga — a long, detailed story; saga is the Viking word for "what is said."

The 1400s were a time of great exploration. Many ships sailed between European ports and Asia. At that time, the only way to get to Asia from Europe was to sail all the way around the southern coast of Africa.

Spanish explorer Christopher Columbus wanted to find a faster way to Asia. In 1492, he sailed from Spain in his flagship, the Santa Maria. After two months at sea, he found land. Columbus believed he'd found a quicker route to Asia. He actually stumbled upon the Caribbean Islands off the southeast coast of North America.

Columbus discovered the New World.

Amazing!

How can he discover it if people already live there?

Millions of Native Americans already lived in North America when Columbus arrived. Europeans didn't know North America existed until Columbus told them about it. They called North America the New World.

By the 1500s, Spanish adventurers, called conquistadors, arrived to explore North and South America. An African slave named Estevanico traveled with Spanish expeditions into the southwestern United States. Estevanico and the Spanish may have been the first non-Native Americans to enter the area now known as Arizona.

Let's go. There's sun, sand, and cactuses to explore.

You go ahead, Estevanico. We'll wait here until someone invents air conditioning.

GREEDY FOR GOLD

Columbus and other early explorers believed the land in North America was loaded with gold. They searched everywhere hoping to become rich. In reality, not much gold was found. But their greed caused these explorers to treat Native Americans with cruelty. They often killed them or took them as slaves.

EARLY SETTLERS

Soon Europeans poured into North America. In 1607, the first successful English settlement in America was founded in Jamestown, Virginia. It was founded on land controlled by the Powhatan Nation of Native Americans.

At first, the Powhatan gave gifts and traded food for copper items with the new immigrants. But Virginia was going through a drought. Soon the Powhatan could not grow enough food to meet the settlers' needs.

The settlers didn't know how to grow their own food. Starvation and disease spread quickly, killing many of them. Eventually they received help from Europe, and Jamestown flourished. Soon more settlements were established up and down the Atlantic coast.

Many of America's first immigrants were brought against their will as slaves. In the 1600s, slavery was legal. Ships brought people from Africa and the Caribbean to slave markets in North America. These people were sold as slaves to European immigrants. Today the descendants of many of those slaves are now U.S. citizens.

Meanwhile, Native Americans were unwelcome in their own country. They suffered greatly during the years of early immigration that created the United States. Through warfare and broken treaties, Native Americans had most of their land taken away. Much of their culture was destroyed.

The Pilgrims

The Pilgrims were some of the most famous immigrants to arrive in North America. They journeyed across the Atlantic from England in 1620. They had separated from the Church of England and wanted to practice their religion freely. They founded the Plymouth Colony in Massachusetts and are remembered for holding the very first Thanksgiving.

PASSING THROUGH ELLIS ISLAND

At the start of the 1900s, immigration to the United States was at its peak. People immigrated for different reasons. Many Irish and Italians came to escape the poverty of their home countries. Germans often immigrated to buy farmland in the Midwest.

Between 1892 and 1954, most people who immigrated to the United States entered through the same place: Ellis Island, New York.

At Ellis Island, immigrants were examined by U.S. Immigration officials and doctors. Doctors watched to see if people coughed, limped, or showed any other signs of sickness. The station was so busy, doctors only had a few seconds to check for cholera, tuberculosis, and other diseases.

You're healthy. Next!

cholera — a dangerous disease that causes severe sickness and diarrhea

Healthy people were allowed to leave the island and enter the United States. Sick people spent days or weeks in the medical wards on the island.

In the 62 years the immigration station was active, 12 million immigrants passed through Ellis Island. Only about 2 percent of immigrants trying to enter the United States were sent back to their home countries.

FAMOUS IMMIGRANTS

Of the millions of immigrants who passed through Ellis Island, some became famous:

BOB HOPE
ENTERTAINER

CHARLIE CHAPLIN
ACTOR

IRVING BERLIN
COMPOSER

CHARLES ATLAS
BODY BUILDER

CHALLENGES FOR IMMIGRANTS

Finding work was difficult for new immigrants. Many did not have the skills to work in the industrial jobs in America's cities. They worked as laborers building bridges and doing other dangerous jobs. In 1870, an unskilled laborer earned $1.75 for a 10-hour day of work. This amount was barely enough to buy food and pay rent.

Finding a safe place to live was another challenge. In 1900, most immigrants in New York lived in cramped apartments called tenements. These buildings were overcrowded and often filled with rats and other animals.

tenement — a rundown apartment building, especially one that is crowded and in a poor part of a city

To make life easier, immigrants joined together with others from their home country. In cities across America, Chinese immigrants created safe places, called Chinatowns, to practice their cultural traditions. An organization called the Order of the Sons of Italy helped immigrants arriving from Italy.

PREJUDICE

FINDING WORK

FINDING A SAFE HOME

NEW LANGUAGES

TAKING CARE OF FAMILY

prejudice — an opinion about others that is unfair or not based on facts

Although laws have been made to protect newcomers to the United States, immigrants still face problems. They must learn a new language, find a safe place to live and work, and overcome prejudice.

UNFAIR IMMIGRATION LAWS

The Indian Removal Act of 1830 forced 16,000 Cherokee Indians to relocate west of the Mississippi River. Cherokees were forced to march 1,000 miles to their new territory. At least 4,000 Cherokees died on the march, now known as the Trail of Tears.

The Chinese Exclusion Act of 1882 banned Chinese laborers from entering the United States. This law also forbid Chinese immigrants living in the United States from becoming citizens. The law was overturned 61 years later, but there were still limits on Chinese immigration until 1965.

Today, people who want to immigrate to the United States must first apply for permission.

This process begins at the U.S. Embassy in their home country. Many forms need to be filled out. Processing the application can take many months.

embassy — a building where representatives from another country work

Successful applicants receive a document called a visa. This permission slip allows them to come to the United States to live and work. The document is a green-colored card and is commonly known as a "green card." A green card must be renewed every 10 years.

"Green card" – original name, huh?

People with green cards are called lawful permanent residents. They are allowed to live and work in the United States, but they are not yet U.S. citizens. Lawful permanent residents cannot vote in elections or hold public office.

What are you doing?

I'm going to be a citizen soon, so I'm practicing how to hold public office.

Lawful permanent residents can apply to have their husband, wife, and unmarried children immigrate to the United States. People who put a large sum of money into an American business can get an investor visa. This visa will let them immigrate to the United States.

Right this way, Mr. Investor.

The rest of you must wait your turn.

THE LOTTERY

Each year in the United States, 55,000 green cards are up for grabs in the Diversity Visa Lottery Program. Lottery winners get a chance to become lawful permanent residents.

WHY PEOPLE IMMIGRATE

People immigrate for many reasons. Some leave their home country to live with family. Others immigrate because they can find a better job in their new country. For others, immigrating is a chance to make a better life for themselves and their family.

In some countries, many people live in poverty because jobs are difficult to find. Some choose to leave their country in search of work. This trend is called the "push factor," because it is like the people are being pushed out of their home country.

Wealthy countries like the United States have plenty of jobs that need workers. But many U.S. citizens won't take these jobs because they don't pay enough or they are too dangerous.

Hi, we're here for jobs.

Great! We've got openings for gardeners, sanitation workers, or nannies.

JOB CENTER

Um, any openings for pop stars or professional basketball players?

Immigrants are willing to take these jobs because they can often earn more than they would in their home country. This trend is called the "pull factor" because it is like the jobs pull people to richer countries.

War, famine, or political struggles can put people's lives in danger and force them to immigrate. People who try to immigrate to a new country because their lives are in danger are called asylum seekers. If they are allowed to immigrate into the new country, they become refugees.

refugee — a person forced to flee his or her home because of natural disaster or war

For some people, the push factor in their home country is very strong. They will risk their lives to immigrate to a new country without permission.

THE PUSH FACTOR DILEMMA

OBEY THE LAW AND YOUR FAMILY GOES HUNGRY.

BREAK THE LAW AND FEED YOUR FAMILY.

Immigrating without permission is against the law. These people are often called illegal immigrants. They are also called undocumented immigrants because they don't have proper immigration documents like a green card.

Your green card is almost expired.

I'm on my way to get it renewed!

Immigrants can also become undocumented if they stay in the country after their visas expire.

A common way for undocumented immigrants to enter the United States is to cross the border with Mexico. Most of this border runs through desert and is very dangerous to cross on foot. Each year, hundreds of people die from harsh desert conditions while trying to cross the border.

The U.S. government built tall fences along parts of the border between Mexico and the United States. The fences are meant to stop people from coming into the United States illegally. Guards patrol the U.S. border and try to stop people from crossing into the country illegally.

REMOVAL

If people who enter the United States illegally are caught, they are taken out of the country. Sending people back used to be called deportation, but now the U.S. government calls it removal.

Becoming citizens of their new country is the goal for many immigrants. In 2006, more than 700,000 people became U.S. citizens.

Congratulations! You are now all U.S. citizens.

The process of becoming a U.S. citizen is called naturalization. U.S. citizenship allows immigrants to vote in elections, serve on a jury in a court trial, and hold political office.

To become citizens, permanent residents must have lived in the United States for at least five years. They must be able to read, write, and speak English. They must also agree to follow the laws of the United States.

Sir, you arrived in the United States yesterday. You can't apply for citizenship for another four years and 364 days.

That's okay. I'll wait here.

Potential citizens must also know United States history and how the U.S. government works. And they have to pass a test to prove it.

I'm so nervous I forgot how to spell U.S.A.

The naturalization test is made up of 10 questions about U.S. history and government. A person needs to get six questions right to pass the test and become a U.S. citizen.

TEST YOUR KNOWLEDGE

The U.S. citizenship test has a variety of questions about U.S. history, government, and politics. Here are a few sample questions to test your knowledge:

1. Why are there 100 senators in the United States Senate?

2. What is the executive of a state government called?

3. When was the Declaration of Independence adopted?

4. Name some countries that were our enemies during World War II.

1. Each state elects two senators; 2. Governor; 3. July 4, 1776; 4. Germany, Italy, and Japan

The United States was built by the hard work of immigrants from around the world. It still is today. Look around and you will see the benefits of immigration.

In 2006, the U.S. government did a study on immigration. It found that legal immigration is good for the country's economy.

The report said that the U.S. economy creates more jobs than can be filled by U.S. citizens. Immigrants fill these jobs and help the United States be more productive. They make the country wealthier and improve living conditions for many Americans.

Immigrants also help the U.S. government and businesses get along with other countries. They can teach the government and businesses about traditions and opportunities in their home countries. Immigrants help the United States trade with countries around the world.

It's a deal!

U.S.A.

JAPAN

But immigrants bring more than political and economic benefits to the United States. If you like pizza, burritos, rice, or falafel, then you've tasted the benefits of immigration. These foods, and many others, were first brought to America by immigrants to the United States. See how many other immigration influences you can find in your home, school, or neighborhood.

Mmm, immigration tastes delicious!

HIGH-TECH IMMIGRANTS

Immigrants are responsible for creating many high-tech businesses, such as Google and Sun Microsystems. Sabeer Bhatia, from India, invented an e-mail program called Hotmail. He later sold it to Microsoft for a reported $400 million.

As long as there are push and pull factors in the world, people will immigrate to new countries. They will continue to search for a place to live a better life.

Many immigrants try to eliminate the push factors of poverty by investing money in their home countries. Some Mexican migrant workers send money they've earned in the United States to home associations in their home country.

The associations use the money to pave roads, invest in factories, build churches, and more. These projects create jobs and reduce poverty in Mexican communities.

Whether they realize it or not, American citizens rely on immigrants every day. Everything from the clothes people wear to the food they eat is made possible because of the hard work of immigrants. These workers were pulled to the United States because of the need for people to fill jobs.

CELL PHONES DESIGNED, SOLD, AND SERVICED BY U.S. IMMIGRANTS

COFFEE BREWED AND SERVED BY U.S. IMMIGRANTS

GROCERIES MADE, SHIPPED, AND SOLD BY U.S. IMMIGRANTS

FRUITS AND VEGETABLES GROWN, PICKED, AND PACKED BY U.S. IMMIGRANTS

CLOTHES DESIGNED AND SOLD BY U.S. IMMIGRANTS

The United States is a nation of immigrants. It will continue to welcome others who want to join the melting pot of America.

WELCOME

TIME LINE

40,000–15,000 BC — The very first immigrants arrive in North America. They spread out over the entire continent to create the Native American nations.

AD 1000 — The Vikings land in present-day Newfoundland, Canada. They make contact with the Inuit people living in the area.

AD 1000

40,000–15,000 BC

1882 — The Chinese Exclusion Act of 1882 bans Chinese laborers from entering the United States. It also prevents Chinese immigrants living in the United States from becoming citizens. The law stays in effect for more than 60 years.

1620 — The Pilgrims arrive from England and create the Plymouth Colony in Massachusetts.

1620

1892 — Ellis Island Immigration Station opens to process the thousands of European immigrants arriving to the U.S. each year. More than 12 million immigrants pass through Ellis Island during its 62 years of operation.

1882

1892

ELLIS ISLAND

1492 — Christopher Columbus arrives in North America. Europeans begin pouring into the New World and settling the Native Americans' lands.

1492

1607 — The first successful English settlement in America is founded in Jamestown, Virginia.

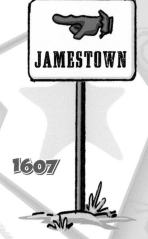

1607

1619 — The first African slaves arrive in Jamestown, Virginia. For more than 200 years, slave ships continue to bring African slaves to America.

1619

2006 — The Secure Fence Act of 2006 is passed. The act allows for 700 miles of fence to be built along the border between Mexico and the United States. The fence is meant to slow the number of illegal immigrants crossing into the United States.

1952 — The Immigration and Nationality Act is passed. It allows people of all races to become citizens.

2006

1952

GLOSSARY

ancestor (AN-sess-tur) — a family member who lived a long time ago

cholera (KOL-ur-uh) — a dangerous disease that causes severe sickness and diarrhea

civilization (si-vuh-luh-ZAY-shuhn) — an organized and advanced society

conquistador (kon-KEYS-tuh-dor) — a leader in the Spanish conquest of North and South America during the 1500s

descendant (di-SEN-duhnt) — a person's child and a family member born after that child

embassy (EM-buh-see) — a building where representatives from another country work

naturalization (nach-ur-uh-luh-ZAY-shuhn) — the process of giving citizenship to someone who was born in another country

prejudice (PREJ-uh-diss) — an opinion about others that is unfair or not based on facts

refugee (ref-yuh-JEE) — a person forced to flee his or her home because of natural disaster or war

saga (SAH-gah) — a long, detailed story; saga is the Viking word for "what is said."

tenement (TEN-uh-muhnt) — a rundown apartment building, especially one that is crowded and in a poor part of a city

tuberculosis (tu-BUR-kyoo-low-sis) — a disease caused by bacteria that causes fever, weight loss, and coughing

visa (VEE-zuh) — a document giving a person permission to enter a foreign country

READ MORE

Britton, Tamara L. *Ellis Island.* Symbols, Landmarks, and Monuments. Edina, Minn.: ABDO, 2004.

Hanel, Rachael. *Mexican Immigrants in America: An Interactive History Adventure.* You Choose Books. Mankato, Minn.: Capstone Press, 2009.

Skog, Jason. *Citizenship.* Cartoon Nation. Mankato, Minn.: Capstone Press, 2008.

Teichmann, Iris. *Life as an Immigrant.* Understanding Immigration. North Mankato, Minn.: Smart Apple Media, 2007.

Wilson, Ruth. *Immigration: A Look at the Way the World Is Today.* Issues of the World. Mankato, Minn.: Stargazer Books, 2006.

INTERNET SITES

FactHound offers a safe, fun way to find Internet sites related to this book. All of the sites on FactHound have been researched by our staff.

Here's how:
1. Visit *www.facthound.com*
2. Choose your grade level.
3. Type in this book ID 142961983X for age-appropriate sites. You may also browse subjects by clicking on letters, or by clicking on pictures and words.
4. Click on the Fetch It button.

FactHound will fetch the best sites for you!

INDEX